Social media emoticons are everywhere, so why not include them in crochet! Choose from 18 blocks showing your favorite emoji, or use the Design-a-Face eyes, mouths, and other features to create your own. The corner-to-corner blocks are fun for making a scarf or blanket, and the facial features have endless possibilities.

Faces 2
Blanket 5
Scarf 10
Design A Face 11
Beanie 18
Slouchy Hat 21
Tissue Box Cover 24
Organizer 26
General Instructions .. 29
Yarn Information 32

LEISURE ARTS, INC. • Maumelle, Arkansas

Faces

●●○○ EASY +

Each face is charted as an Emoji Squares. Any of the 18 squares can be used for the Blanket on page 5 or the Scarf on page 9. Refer to the yarn colors below.

SHOPPING LIST

Yarn

Colors needed to make all Faces:

Background Color

- ☐ Dark Blue

Face Colors

- ☐ Yellow
- ☐ Brown
- ☐ Black
- ☐ Blue
- ☐ White
- ☐ Dark Pink
- ☐ Pink
- ☐ Grey

Crochet Hook

- ☐ See Blanket on page 5 or Scarf on page 9.

Additional Supplies

- ☐ Bobbins

GAUGE INFORMATION

See Blanket or Scarf for gauge information.

STITCH GUIDE

BEGINNING BLOCK

Ch 6, turn; dc in fourth ch from hook and in next 2 chs.

BLOCK

Slip st in ch-3 sp on next Block ***(Fig. A)***, ch 3, 3 dc in same sp ***(Fig. B)***.

Fig. A

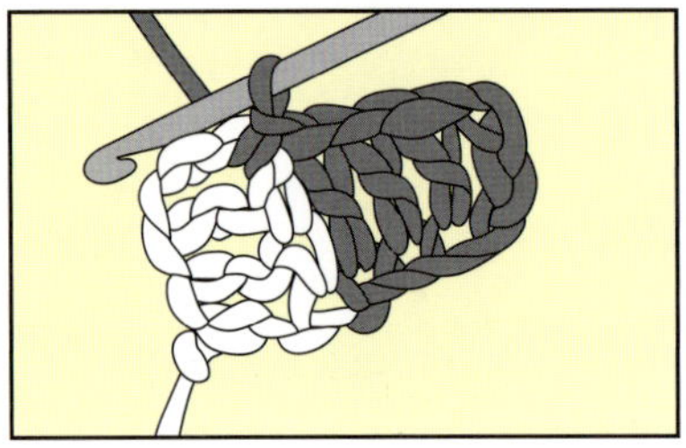

Fig. B

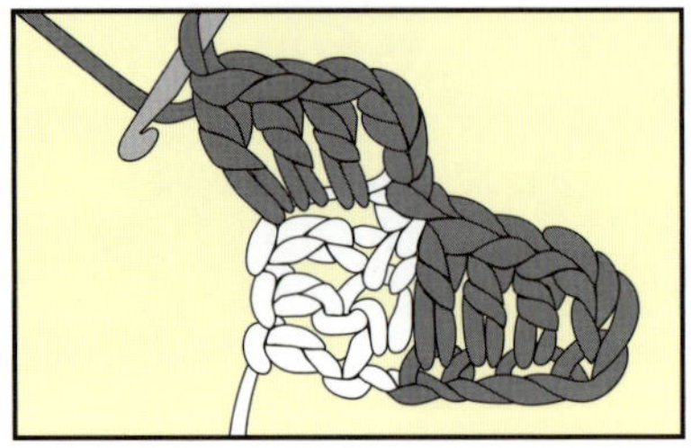

Each Square is worked diagonally.

EMOJI SQUARE

SMILEY FACE

Row 1 (Right side)**:** With Dark Blue, ch 6, dc in fourth ch from hook and in next 2 ch: one Block.

Note: Loop a short piece of yarn around any stitch to mark Row 1 as **right** side **and** bottom corner.

Row 2: Work Beginning Block, slip st in ch-3 sp on previous Block, ch 3, 3 dc in same sp: 2 Blocks.

Row 3: Work Beginning Block, slip st in ch-3 sp on first Block, ch 3, 3 dc in same sp, work Block: 3 Blocks.

Rows 4 and 5: Work Beginning Block, slip st in ch-3 sp on first Block, ch 3, 3 dc in same sp, work Blocks across: 5 Blocks.

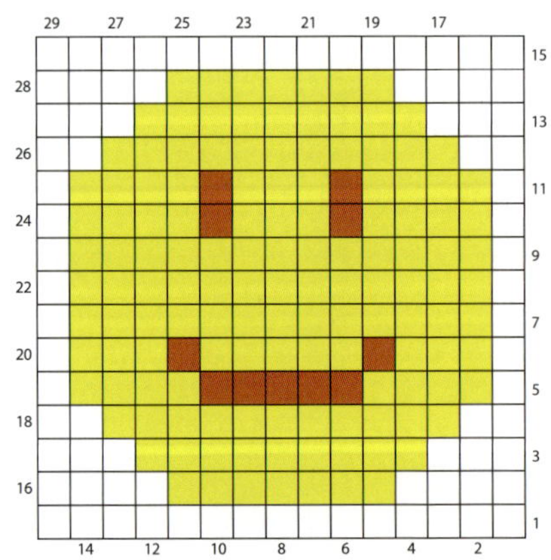

Smiley Face

Row 6: Work Beginning Block changing to Yellow in last dc made *(Fig. C)*, slip st in ch-3 sp on first Block, ch 3, 3 dc in same sp, work 2 Blocks, work Block changing to second Dark Blue in last dc, work Block: 6 Blocks.

Fig. C

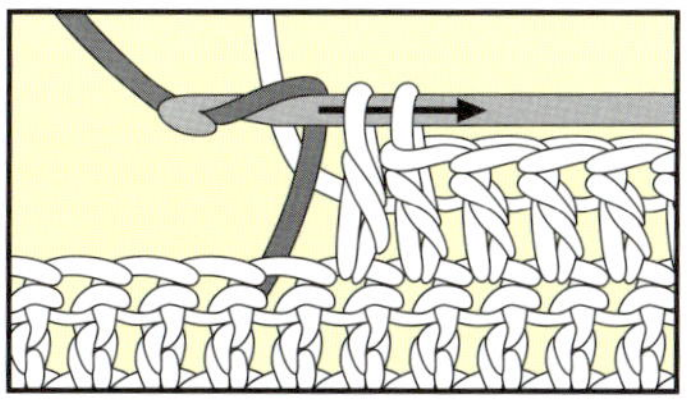

Always change colors in same manner, using bobbins for small sections of color. Keep unused color to **wrong** side of work; do **not** cut yarn until color is no longer needed.

Row 7: Work Beginning Block, with Yellow, slip st in ch-3 sp on first Block, ch 3, 3 dc in same sp, work 4 Blocks, with second Dark Blue, work Block: 7 Blocks.

Rows 8-15: Follow Chart.

Rows 16-27: Turn; slip st in first 3 dc and in next ch-3 sp, ch 3, 3 dc in same sp, following chart work Blocks across to last Block, slip st in ch-3 sp on last Block: 3 Blocks.

Row 28: Turn; slip st in first 3 dc and in next ch-3 sp, ch 3, 3 dc in same sp, work Block, slip st in ch-3 sp on last Block: 2 Blocks.

ADDITIONAL SQUARES

Follow chart for desired Squares.

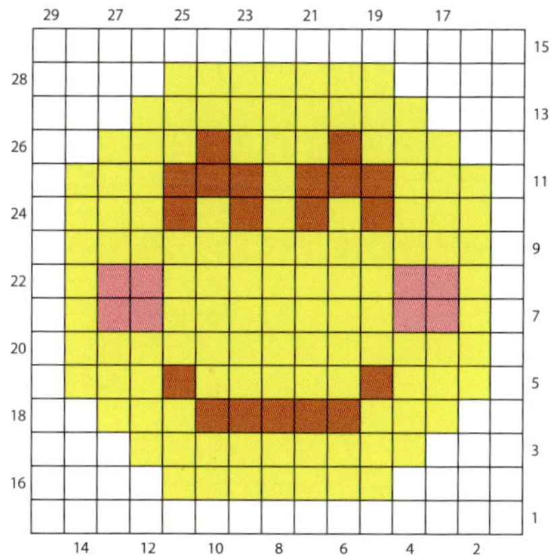

Blush Smile

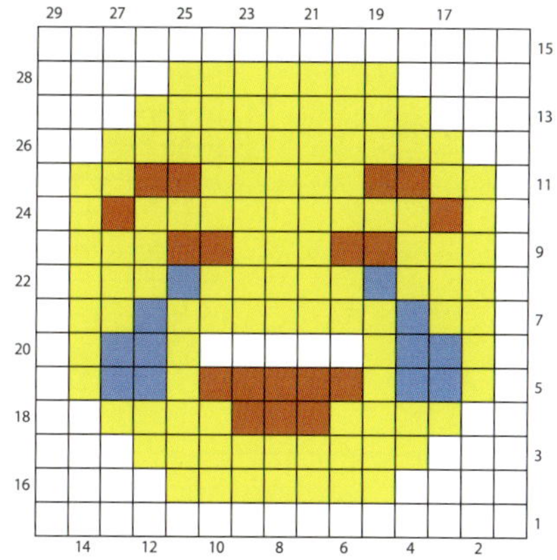

Tears of Joy

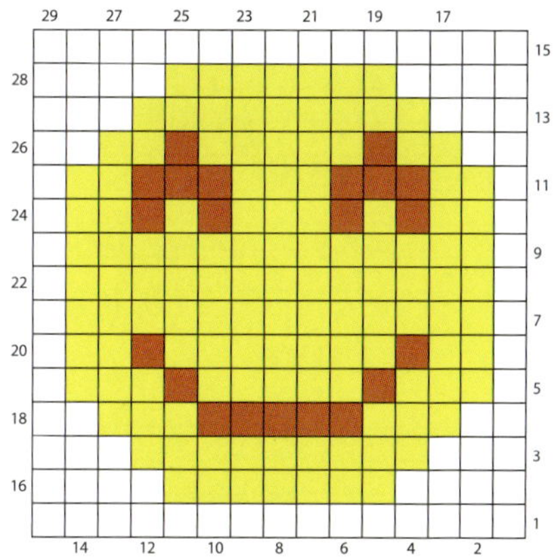

Smiling Eyes

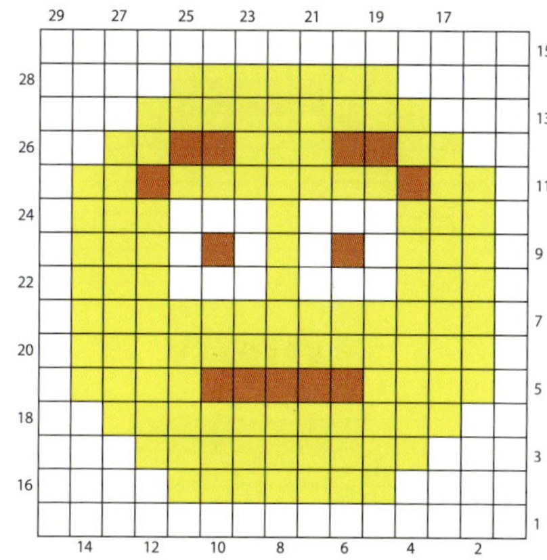

Awkward

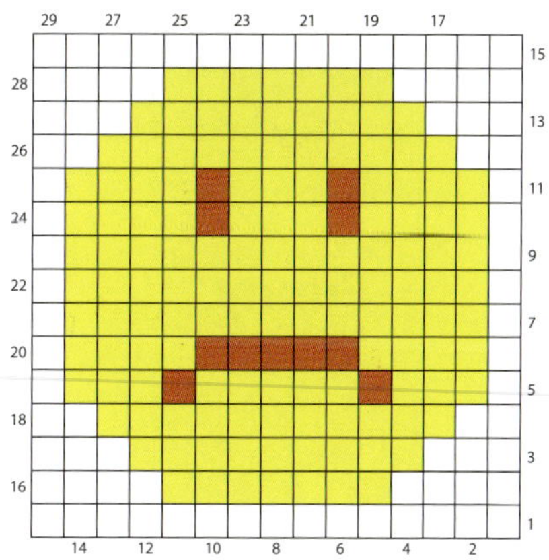

Frown

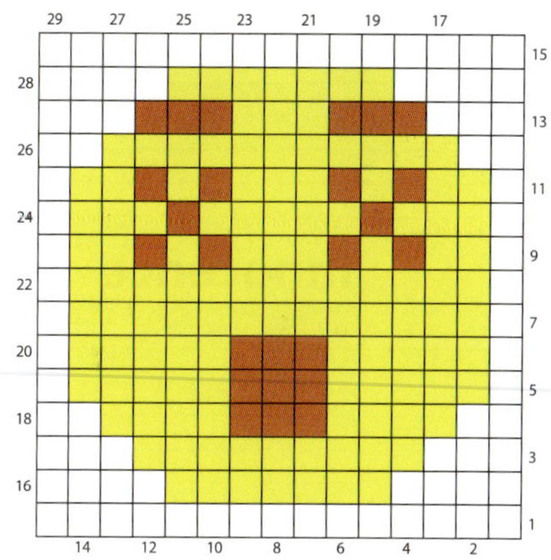

Shocked

Row 29: Turn; slip st in first 3 dc and in next ch-3 sp, ch 3, 3 dc in same sp, slip st in ch-3 sp on last Block, finish off: one Block.

Note: To make features more continuous, thread a yarn needle with color needed and make a few stitches to connect Blocks.

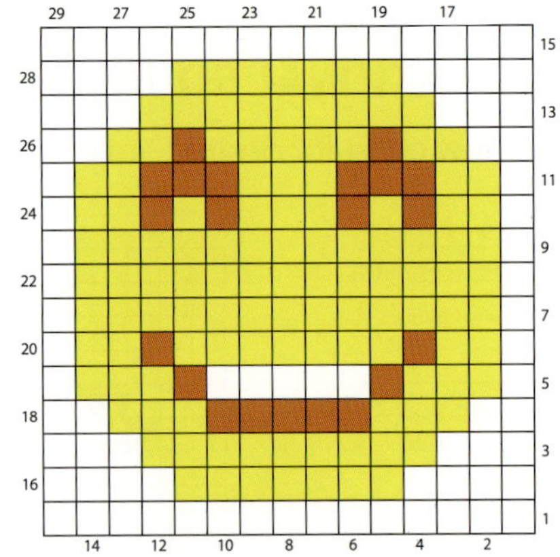

Big Smile

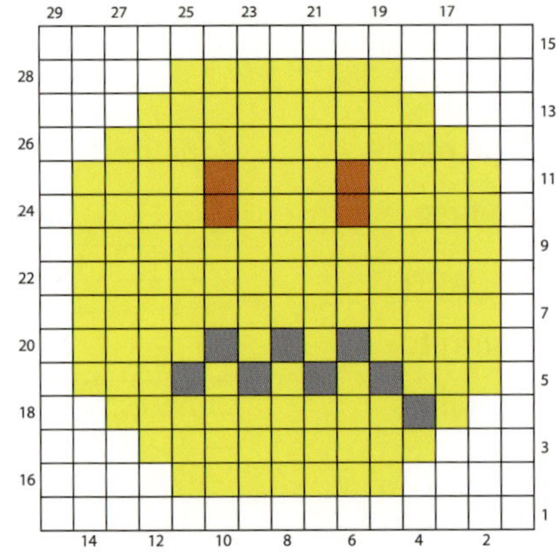

Zipped Lips

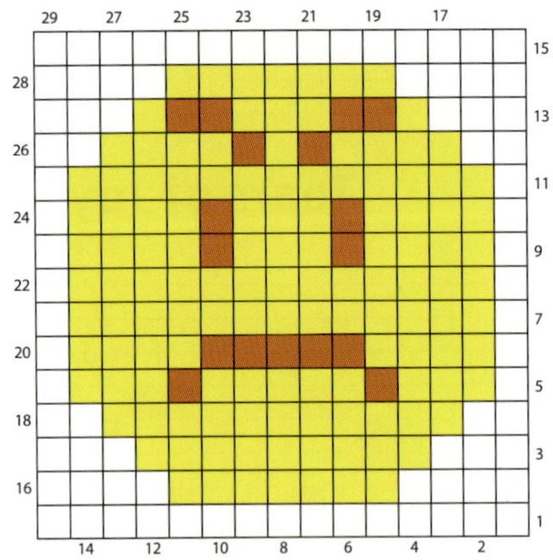

Angry

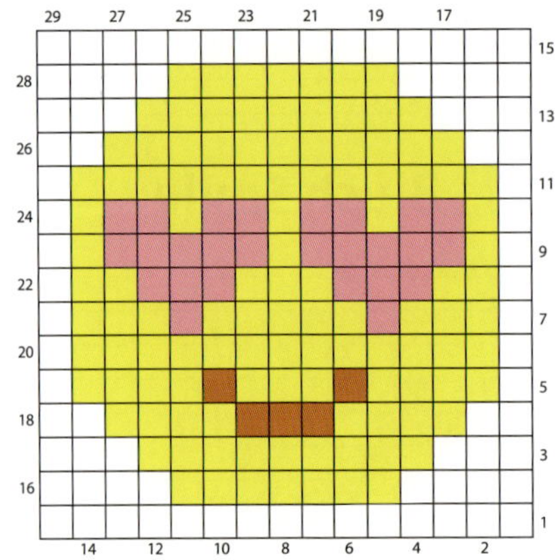

Love

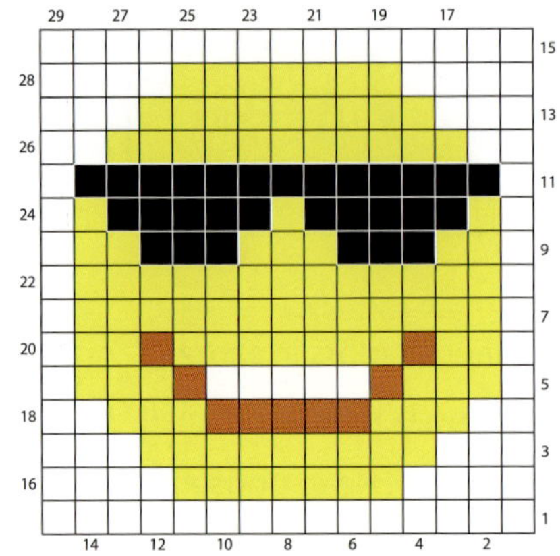

Joe Cool

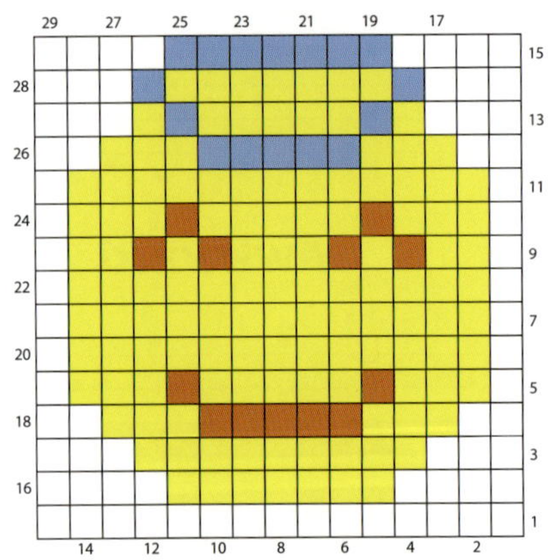

Innocence

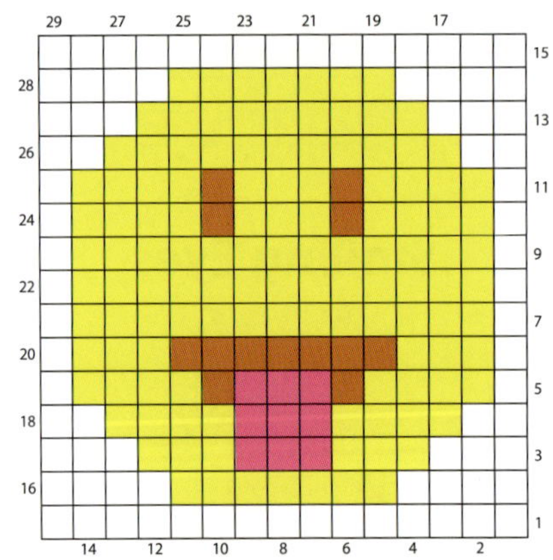

Funny

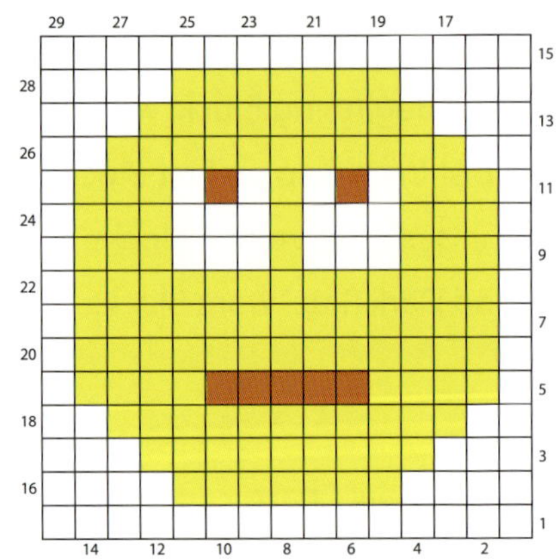

Eye Roll

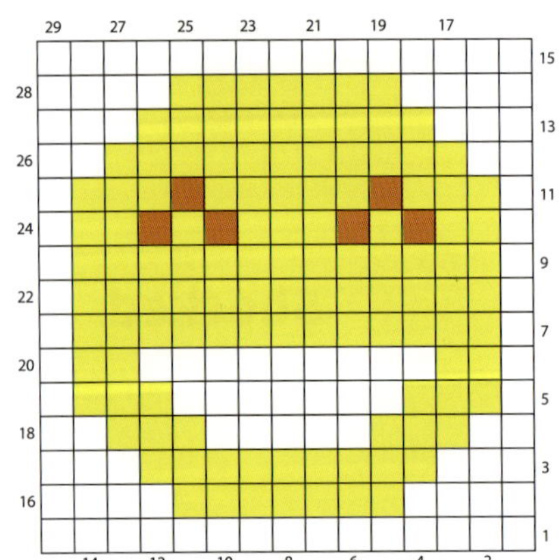

Happy Grin

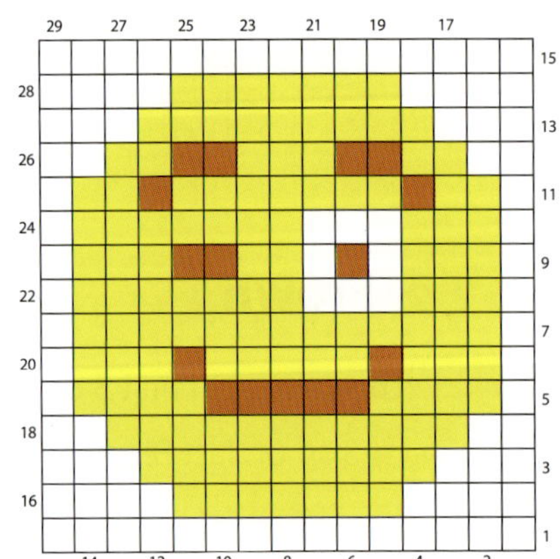

Wink

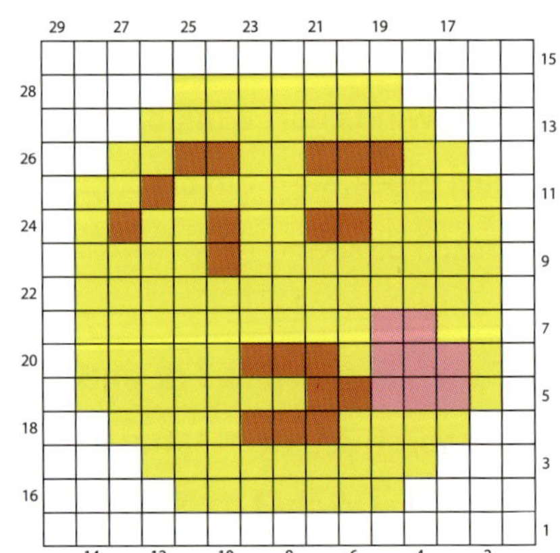

Blowing a Kiss

Blanket

Shown on page 8.

●●○○ EASY +

SHOPPING LIST

Yarn (Medium Weight) MEDIUM 4

[7 ounces, 370 yards
(198 grams, 338 meters) per skein]:

- ☐ Dark Blue - 4 skeins
- ☐ Brown - 60 yards (55 meters)
- ☐ White - 30 yards (27.5 meters)
- ☐ Pink - 20 yards (18.5 meters)
- ☐ Blue - 20 yards (18.5 meters)
- ☐ Black - 20 yards (18.5 meters)
- ☐ Dark Pink - 5 yards (4.5 meters)

[7 ounces, 364 yards
(198 grams, 333 meters) per skein]:

- ☐ Yellow - 2 skeins

Crochet Hook

- ☐ Size G (4 mm)
  or size needed for gauge

Additional Supplies

- ☐ Bobbins
- ☐ Yarn needle

SIZE INFORMATION

Finished Sizes:

Child Size: 39" x 48¾"
(99 cm x 124 cm)

Full Size: 48¾" x 58½"
(124 cm x 148.5 cm)

Size Note: We have printed the instructions for the sizes in different colors to make it easier for you to find:

- Child Size in Blue
- Full Size in Pink

Instructions in Black apply to both sizes.

GAUGE INFORMATION

In pattern, 5 Blocks = 3¼" (8.25 cm)
Each Square = 9¾" (24.75 cm)

Gauge Swatch: 3¼" x 3¼" x 4½"
(8.25 cm x 8.25 cm x 10.75 cm)

Work same as Square for 5 rows.

STITCH GUIDE

BEGINNING BLOCK

Ch 6, turn; dc in fourth ch from hook and in next 2 chs.

BLOCK

Slip st in ch-3 sp on next Block, ch 3, 3 dc in same sp *(Figs. A & B, page 2)*.

Each Square is worked diagonally.

SOLID SQUARE [Make 10{15}]

Row 1 (Right side)**:** With Dark Blue, ch 6, dc in fourth ch from hook and in next 2 chs: one Block.

Note: Loop a short piece of yarn around any stitch to mark Row 1 as **right** side **and** bottom corner.

Row 2: Work Beginning Block, slip st in ch-3 sp on previous Block, ch 3, 3 dc in same sp: 2 Blocks.

Row 3: Work Beginning Block, slip st in ch-3 sp on first Block, ch 3, 3 dc in same sp, work Block: 3 Blocks.

Rows 4-15: Work Beginning Block, slip st in ch-3 sp on first Block, ch 3, 3 dc in same sp, work Blocks across: 15 Blocks.

Rows 16-27: Turn; slip st in first 3 dc and in next ch-3 sp, ch 3, 3 dc in same sp, work Blocks across to last Block, slip st in ch-3 sp on last Block: 3 Blocks.

Row 28: Turn; slip st in first 3 dc and in next ch-3 sp, ch 3, 3 dc in same sp, work Block, slip st in ch-3 sp on last Block: 2 Blocks.

Row 29: Turn; slip st in first 3 dc and in next ch-3 sp, ch 3, 3 dc in same sp, slip st in ch-3 sp on last Block: one Block.

Row 30: Turn; slip st in first 3 dc and in next ch-3 sp; finish off leaving a long for sewing.

EMOJI SQUARE

[Make 10{15}]

Make desired Emoji Squares, pages 2-4.

ASSEMBLY

Using diagram as a guide for placement, Dark Blue, and with **wrong** sides together, sew Squares together forming 4{5} vertical strips of 5{6} Squares **each**; then sew strips together in same manner.

EDGING

Rnd 1: With **right** side facing, join Dark Blue with sc in top corner *(see Joining With Sc, page 30)*; 2 sc in same st, sc evenly around entire Blanket, working 3 sc in each corner; join with slip st to first sc, finish off.

Rnd 2: With **right** side facing, join Yellow with sc in center sc of any corner 3-sc group; 2 sc in same st, sc in each sc around, working 3 sc in center sc of each corner 3-sc group; join with slip st to first sc, finish off.

Rnd 3: With **right** side facing, join Dark Blue with slip st in any sc; ch 1, working from **left** to **right**, ★ insert hook in st to right of hook *(Fig. A)*, YO and draw through, under and to left of loop on hook (2 loops on hook) *(Fig. B)*, YO and draw through both loops on hook *(Fig. C)* **(reverse sc made, *Fig. D*)**; repeat from ★ around; join with slip st to first st, finish off.

Fig. A

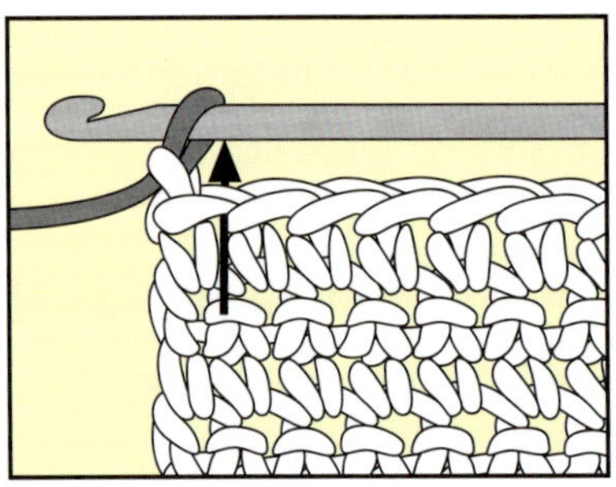

Fig. B

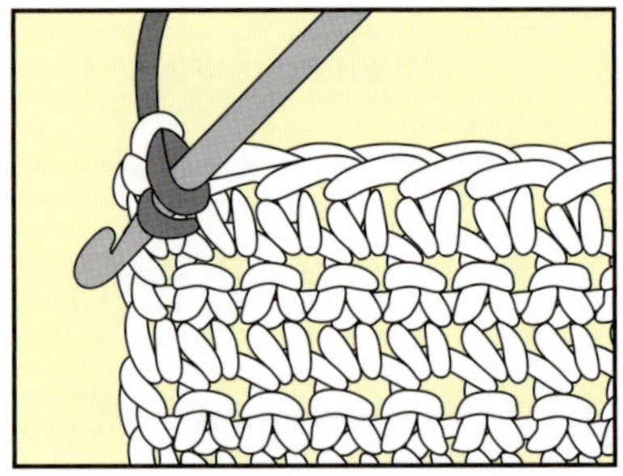

Fig. C

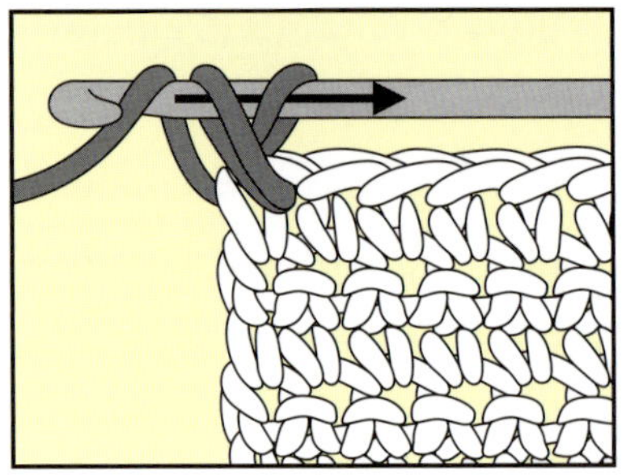

Fig. D

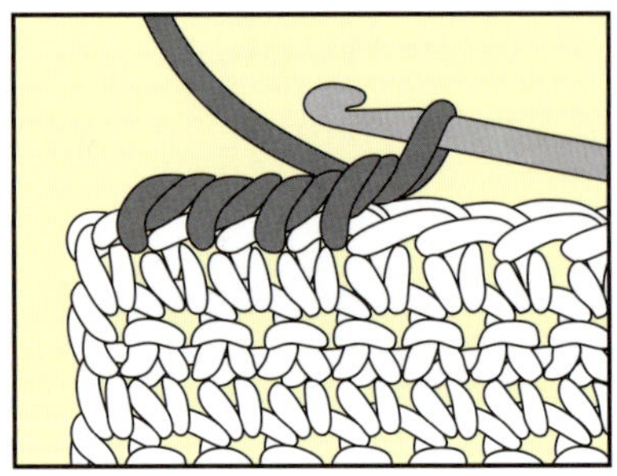

Design by Lois J. Long.

Child Size Blanket Diagram

Emoji	Solid	Emoji	Solid
Solid	Emoji	Solid	Emoji
Emoji	Solid	Emoji	Solid
Solid	Emoji	Solid	Emoji
Emoji	Solid	Emoji	Solid

Full Size Blanket Diagram

Solid	Emoji	Solid	Emoji	Solid
Emoji	Solid	Emoji	Solid	Emoji
Solid	Emoji	Solid	Emoji	Solid
Emoji	Solid	Emoji	Solid	Emoji
Solid	Emoji	Solid	Emoji	Solid
Emoji	Solid	Emoji	Solid	Emoji

Scarf

Shown on page 9.

●●○○ EASY +

Finished Size: 7½" wide x 45" long (19" x 114.5 cm)

SHOPPING LIST

Yarn (Light Weight) LIGHT 3

[3 ounces, 330 yards (85 grams, 301 meters) per skein]:

- ☐ Dark Blue - 1 skein
- ☐ Yellow - 1 skein
- ☐ Brown - 30 yards (27.5 meters)

Crochet Hook

- ☐ Size H (5 mm) **or** size needed for gauge

Additional Supplies

- ☐ Yarn needle

GAUGE INFORMATION

In pattern, 4 Blocks = 2" (5 cm)
Each Square = 7½" (19 cm)
Gauge Swatch: 2½" x 2½" x 3¼" (6.25 cm x 6.25 cm x 8.25 cm)
Work same as Square for 5 rows.

SCARF

EMOJI SQUARE (Make 2)

Make one Smiling Eyes and one Frown Square, pages 2-4.

FIRST HALF

Row 1: With **right** side of either Emoji Square facing and working across top edge, join Dark Blue with sc in first corner *(see Joining With Sc, page 30)*; work 38 sc evenly spaced across: 39 sc.

Row 2: Ch 3 **(counts as first dc, now and throughout)**, turn; dc in next 2 sc, ★ ch 1, skip next sc, dc in next 3 sc; repeat from ★ across: 30 dc and 9 ch-1 sps.

Row 3: Ch 4 **(counts as first dc plus ch 1)**, turn; skip next dc, dc in next dc, ★ dc in next ch-1 sp and in next dc, ch 1, skip next dc, dc in next dc; repeat from ★ across.

Row 4: Ch 3, turn; dc in next ch-1 sp and in next dc, ★ ch 1, skip next dc, dc in next dc, dc in next ch-1 sp and in next dc; repeat from ★ across.

Repeat Rows 3 and 4 for pattern until piece measures 22½" (57 cm) from bottom of Emoji Square, ending by working Row 4; finish off.

SECOND HALF

Row 1: With **right** side of remaining Emoji Square facing and working across top edge, join Dark Blue with sc in first corner; work 38 sc evenly spaced across: 39 sc.

Complete same as First Half, ending by working Row 3 and leaving a long end for sewing.

With **wrong** sides of both pieces together, using long end, and working in **both** loops of **both** pieces, whipstitch pieces together *(Fig. 6, page 31)*.

Design by Lois J. Long.

Design A Face

●●○○ EASY +

Finished Size: 4" (10 cm) diameter

SHOPPING LIST

Yarn (Medium Weight) MEDIUM 4

Colors needed to create all Faces:

See individual pieces for yardage.

- ☐ Yellow
- ☐ Brown
- ☐ Blue
- ☐ White
- ☐ Dark Pink
- ☐ Pink
- ☐ Grey

Crochet Hook

- ☐ Size G (4 mm)

  or size needed for gauge

Additional Supplies

- ☐ Yarn needle

Gauge Swatch: 1¼" (3.25 cm)

Work same as Head through Rnd 3: 18 sc.

HEAD

16 yards (14.5 meters)

Rnd 1 (Right side)**:** With Yellow, ch 2, 6 sc in second ch from hook; do **not** join, place marker to indicate beginning of rnd *(see Markers, page 30)*.

Note: Loop a short piece of yarn around any stitch to mark Rnd 1 as **right** side.

Rnd 2: 2 Sc in each sc around: 12 sc.

Rnd 3: (Sc in next sc, 2 sc in next sc) around: 18 sc.

Rnd 4: (2 Sc in next sc, sc in next 2 sc) around: 24 sc.

Rnd 5: (Sc in next 3 sc, 2 sc in next sc) around: 30 sc.

Rnd 6: Sc in next 3 sc, 2 sc in next sc, (sc in next 4 sc, 2 sc in next sc) 5 times, sc in next sc: 36 sc.

Rnd 7: Sc in next sc, 2 sc in next sc, (sc in next 5 sc, 2 sc in next sc) 5 times, sc in next 4 sc: 42 sc.

Rnd 8: Sc in next 3 sc, 2 sc in next sc, (sc in next 6 sc, 2 sc in next sc) 5 times, sc in next 3 sc: 48 sc.

Rnd 9: (2 Sc in next sc, sc in next 7 sc) around: 54 sc.

Rnd 10: Sc in each sc around; slip st in next sc, finish off leaving a long end for sewing.

OVAL EYES

2 yards (2 meters)

With Brown, ch 4.

Rnd 1 (Right side)**:** 3 Sc in second ch from hook, sc in next ch, 3 sc in last ch; sc in free loop of next ch ***(Fig. 4, page 31)***; join with slip st to first sc: 8 sc.

For Small Oval Eye; finish off.

Note: Mark Rnd 1 as **right** side.

Rnd 2: Ch 1, 2 sc in same st as joining and in each of next 2 sc, sc in next sc, 2 sc in each of next 3 sc, sc in last sc; join with slip st to first sc, finish off leaving a long end for sewing: 14 sc.

ROUND EYE

1 yard (1 meter)

Rnd 1 (Right side)**:** With Brown, ch 2, 6 sc in second ch from hook; slip st in next sc, finish off leaving a long end for sewing: 6 sc.

Note: Mark Rnd 1 as **right** side.

WIDE OPEN EYE

White - 2 yards (2 meters)
Brown - 1 yard (1 meter)

Rnd 1 (Right side)**:** With Brown, make an adjustable loop to form a ring ***(Figs. 1a-d, page 30)***, work 6 sc in ring; cut Brown, with White, join with slip st to first sc ***(Fig. A)***.

Fig. A

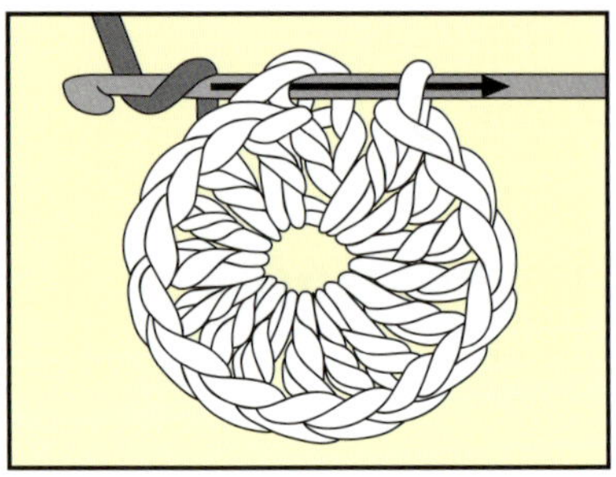

Note: Mark Rnd 1 as **right** side.

Rnd 2: Ch 3 **(counts as first dc)**, dc in same st, 2 dc in next sc and in each sc around; join with slip st to first dc, finish off leaving a long end for sewing: 12 dc.

SAD EYE

1 yard (1 meter)

With Brown, ch 8.

Row 1 (Right side)**:** Working in back ridge of beginning ch *(Fig. 2, page 30)*, slip st in second ch from hook and in each ch across; finish off leaving a long end for sewing.

Note: Mark Row 1 as **right** side.

WINK EYE

1 yard (1 meter)

With Brown, ch 6.

Row 1 (Right side)**:** Working in back ridge of beginning ch *(Fig. 2, page 30)*, sc in second ch from hook and in each ch across; finish off leaving a long end for sewing: 5 sc.

Note: Mark Row 1 as **right** side.

HEART EYE

3 yards (2.75 meters)

With Dark Pink, ch 2.

Row 1: Sc in second ch from hook: one sc.

Row 2 (Right side)**:** Ch 1, turn; 2 sc in first sc: 2 sc.

Note: Mark Row 2 as **right** side.

Row 3: Ch 1, turn; 2 sc in first sc, sc in last sc: 3 sc.

Row 4: Ch 3 **(counts as first dc)**, turn; (dc, sc) in first sc, slip st in next sc, (sc, 2 dc) in last sc: 7 sts.

Trim: Do **not** turn; sc in end of first 3 rows; 3 sc in free loop of beginning ch *(Fig. 4, page 31)*; sc in end of last 3 rows; working across sts on Row 4, sc in first dc, 2 sc in next dc, slip st in next 3 sts, 2 sc in next dc, sc in last dc; join with slip st to first sc, finish off leaving a long end for sewing.

SMILE

3 yards (2.75 meters)

With Brown, ch 20.

Row 1 (Right side)**:** Working in back ridge of beginning ch *(Fig. 2, page 30)*, slip st in second ch from hook and in next ch, sc in next 3 chs, hdc in next 3 chs, dc in next 3 chs, hdc in next 3 chs, sc in next 3 chs, slip st in last 2 chs; finish off leaving a long end for sewing: 19 sts.

Note: Mark Row 1 as **right** side.

FROWN/SMALL SMILE

3 yards (2.75 meters)

With Brown, ch 14.

Row 1 (Right side)**:** Working in back ridge of beginning ch *(Fig. 2, page 30)*, slip st in second ch from hook, sc in next 2 chs, hdc in next 2 chs, dc in next 3 chs, hdc in next 2 chs, sc in next 2 chs, slip st in last ch; finish off leaving a long end for sewing: 13 sts.

Note: Mark Row 1 as **right** side.

WIDE OPEN MOUTH

3 yards (2.75 meters)

Rnd 1 (Right side)**:** With Brown, ch 2, 6 sc in second ch from hook; do **not** join, place marker to indicate beginning of rnd *(see Markers, page 30)*.

Note: Mark Rnd 1 as **right** side.

Rnd 2: 2 Sc in each sc around: 12 sc.

Rnd 3: (Sc in next sc, 2 sc in next sc) around; slip st in next sc, finish off leaving a long end for sewing: 18 sc.

ZIPPED MOUTH

1 yard (1 meter)

Row 1 (Right side)**:** With Grey, ch 2, sc in second ch from hook, ch 3, sc in second ch from hook, skip last ch, ch 3, (sc, ch 1, slip st) in second ch from hook; working along opposite side, ch 2, sc in second ch from hook, ★ slip st in next unworked ch and in same ch as next sc, ch 2, sc in second ch from hook; repeat from ★ once **more**, slip st in in same ch as first sc made, ch 4, 2 hdc in second ch from hook, slip st in last 2 chs **(tab made)**; finish off leaving a long end for sewing.

Note: Mark Row 1 as **right** side.

TONGUE

3 yards (2.75 meters)

With Dark Pink, ch 6.

Row 1: Sc in second ch from hook and in next 3 chs, 3 sc in last ch; working in free loops of beginning ch *(Fig. 4, page 31)*, sc in next 4 chs; do **not** join: 11 sc.

Trim (Right side)**:** Ch 1, turn; sc in first 4 sc, 2 sc in next sc, 3 sc in next sc, 2 sc in next sc, sc in next 3 sc, 2 sc in last sc; skip end of Row 1, sc in same ch as first sc, skip end of Row 1, sc in same sc as first sc; join with slip st to first sc, finish off leaving a long end for sewing: 18 sc.

Note: Mark Trim as **right** side.

LONG TONGUE

3½ yards (3.25 meters)

With Dark Pink, ch 8.

Row 1: Sc in second ch from hook and in next 5 chs, 3 sc in last ch; working in free loops of beginning ch *(Fig. 4, page 31)*, sc in next 6 chs; do **not** join: 15 sc.

Trim (Right side)**:** Ch 1, turn; sc in first 6 sc, 2 sc in next sc, 3 sc in next sc, 2 sc in next sc, sc in next 5 sc, 2 sc in last sc; skip end of Row 1, sc in same ch as first sc, skip end of Row 1, sc in same sc as first sc; join with slip st to first sc, finish off leaving a long end for sewing: 22 sc.

Note: Mark Trim as **right** side.

TEARDROP

2 yards (2 meters)

With Blue, ch 4.

Rnd 1 (Right side)**:** (2 Hdc, sc) in second ch from hook, sc in next ch, (slip st, ch 1, slip st) in last ch; working in free loops of beginning ch *(Fig. 4, page 31)*, sc in next ch, (sc, hdc) in next ch; join with slip st to first hdc, finish off leaving a long end for sewing: 10 sts.

Note: Mark Rnd 1 as **right** side.

LARGE TEARDROP

2 yards (2 meters)

With Blue, ch 6.

Rnd 1 (Right side)**:** (2 Dc, hdc) in third ch from hook, hdc in next ch, sc in next ch, (slip st, ch 1, slip st) in last ch; working in free loops of beginning ch *(Fig. 4, page 31)*, sc in next ch, hdc in next ch, (hdc, dc) in next ch; join with slip st to first dc, finish off leaving a long end for sewing: 12 sts.

Note: Mark Rnd 1 as **right** side.

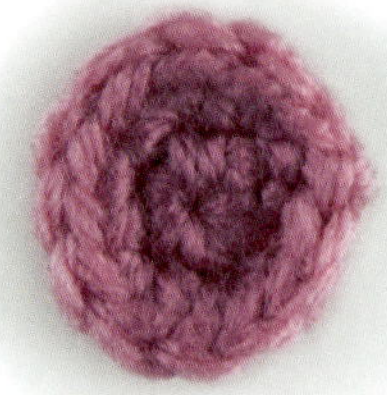

CHEEK

2 yards (2 meters)

Rnd 1 (Right side)**:** With Pink, ch 2, 6 sc in second ch from hook; do **not** join, place marker to indicate beginning of rnd *(see Markers, page 30)*.

Note: Mark Rnd 1 as **right** side.

Rnd 2: 2 Sc in each sc around; slip st in next sc, finish off leaving a long end for sewing: 12 sc.

MASK

15 yards (13.5 meters)

BODY

With White, ch 13, place marker in second ch from hook for Strap placement.

Row 1 (Wrong side)**:** Sc in second ch from hook and in each ch across: 12 sc.

Note: Mark the **back** of any stitch on Row 1 as **right** side.

Rows 2-7: Ch 1, turn; sc in each sc across; do **not** finish off.

TRIM AND STRAPS

Ch 1, turn; sc in each sc across, ch 6, sc in back ridge of second ch from hook *(Fig. 2, page 30)* and each ch across (**Strap made**), sc in same st as last sc on Row 7; sc in end of next 6 rows; working in free loops of beginning ch *(Fig. 4, page 31)*, sc in marked ch, † ch 6, sc in back ridge of second ch from hook and each ch across (**Strap made**), sc in same ch at base of Strap †, sc in each sc across, repeat from † to † once; sc in end of next 6 row and in same sc as first sc, ch 6, sc in back ridge of second ch from hook and each ch across (**Strap made**); join with slip st to first sc, finish off.

SMALL MASK

6 yards (5.5 meters)

BODY

With White, ch 10, place marker in second ch from hook for Strap placement.

Row 1 (Wrong side)**:** Sc in second ch from hook and in each ch across: 9 sc.

Note: Mark the **back** of any stitch on Row 1 as **right** side.

Rows 2-5: Ch 1, turn; sc in each sc across; do **not** finish off.

TRIM AND STRAPS

Ch 1, turn; sc in each sc across, ch 6, sc in back ridge of second ch from hook *(Fig. 2, page 30)* and each ch across (**Strap made**), sc in same st as last sc on Row 5; sc in end of next 4 rows; working in free loops of beginning ch *(Fig. 4, page 31)*, sc in marked ch, † ch 3, sc in back ridge of second ch from hook and next ch (**Strap made**), sc in same ch at base of Strap †, sc in each sc across, repeat from † to † once; sc in end of next 4 rows and in same sc as first sc, ch 6, sc in back ridge of second ch from hook and each ch across (**Strap made**); join with slip st to first sc, finish off.

Designs by Lois J. Long.

Beanie

●●○○ EASY

SHOPPING LIST

Yarn (Medium Weight) MEDIUM 4

[16 ounces, 1,020 yards

(454 grams, 932 meters) per skein]:

☐ Yellow - 160 yards

(146.5 meters)

See pages 12-17 for colors and yardage of desired features.

Crochet Hook

☐ Size H (5 mm)

or size needed for gauge

Additional Supplies

☐ Yarn needle

GAUGE INFORMATION

In pattern,

16 sts and 7 rnds = 4" (10 cm)

Gauge Swatch:

3½" (9 cm) diameter

Work same as Body through Rnd 3: 36 dc.

SIZE INFORMATION

Size: Small{Medium-Large}

19{21-23}"/48.5{53.5-58.5} cm

Size Note: We have printed the instructions for the sizes in different colors to make it easier for you to find:

- Size Small in Blue
- Medium in Pink
- Size Large in Green

Instructions in Black apply to all sizes.

BODY

With Yellow, ch 4; join with slip st to form a ring.

Rnd 1 (Right side)**:** Ch 1, (sc, hdc, 10 dc) in ring; do **not** join, place marker to indicate beginning of rnd ***(see Markers, page 30)***: 12 sts.

Work in Back Loops Only throughout ***(Fig. 3, page 30)***.

Rnd 2: 2 Dc in each st around: 24 dc.

Rnd 3: (Dc in next dc, 2 dc in next dc) around: 36 dc.

Rnd 4: (Dc in next 2 dc, 2 dc in next dc) around: 48 dc.

Rnd 5: (Dc in next 3 dc, 2 dc in next dc) around: 60 dc.

Rnd 6: (Dc in next 4 dc, 2 dc in next dc) around: 72 dc.

Size Small ONLY

Rnd 7: Dc in each dc around.

Repeat Rnd 7 until Body measures approximately 10" (25.5 cm) from beginning ring.

Next Rnd: Dc in next 68 dc, hdc in next 2 dc, sc in next 2 dc.

Last Rnd: Sc in each st around; slip st in next sc, finish off.

Size Medium ONLY

Rnd 7: (Dc in next 5 dc, 2 dc in next dc) around: 84 dc.

Rnd 8: Dc in each dc around.

Repeat Rnd 8 until Body measures approximately 10½" (26.5 cm) from beginning ring.

Next Rnd: Dc in next 80 dc, hdc in next 2 dc, sc in next 2 dc.

Last Rnd: Sc in each st around; slip st in next sc, finish off.

Size Large ONLY

Rnd 7: (Dc in next 5 dc, 2 dc in next dc) around: 84 dc.

Rnd 8: ★ Dc in next 10 dc, 2 dc in next dc, dc in next 9 dc, 2 dc in next dc; repeat from ★ around: 92 dc.

Rnd 9: Dc in each dc around.

Repeat Rnd 9 until Body measures approximately 11" (28 cm) from beginning ring.

Next Rnd: Dc in next 88 dc, hdc in next 2 dc, sc in next 2 dc.

Last Rnd: Sc in each st around; slip st in next sc, finish off.

Make desired features on pages 12-17; then sew to Beanie.

POM-POM

Cut a piece of cardboard 3" wide x 2½" (long 7.5 cm x 6.5 cm) .
Wind Yellow around the cardboard until it is approximately ½" (12 mm) thick in the middle *(Fig. A)*.
Carefully slip the yarn off the cardboard and firmly tie an 18" (45.5 cm) length of yarn around the middle *(Fig. B)*. Leave yarn ends long enough to attach the pom-pom. Cut the loops on both ends and trim the pom-pom into a smooth ball *(Fig. C)*.

Attach to top of hat.

Design by Lisa Gentry.

Fig. A

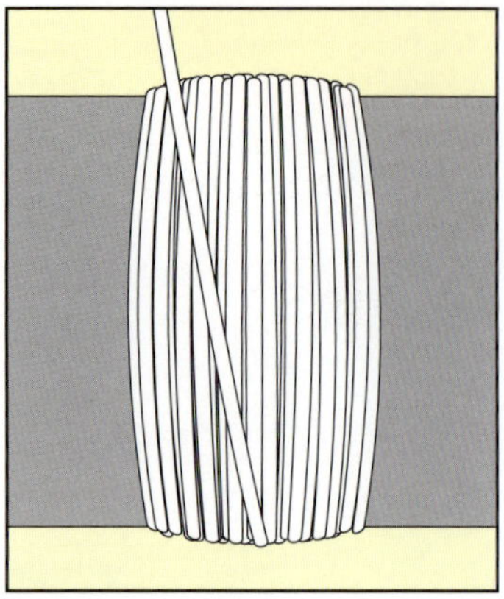

Fig. B

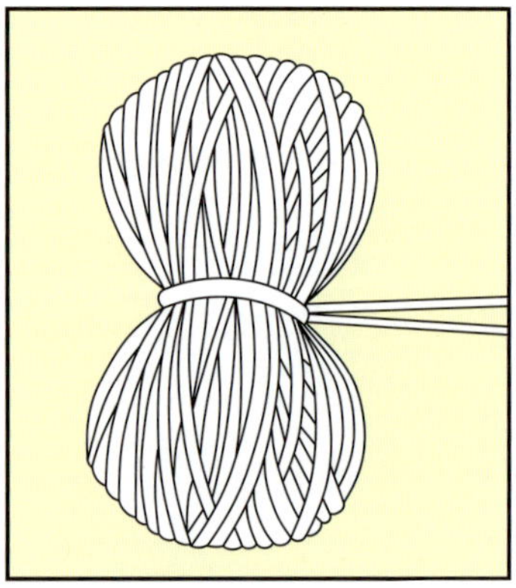

Fig. C

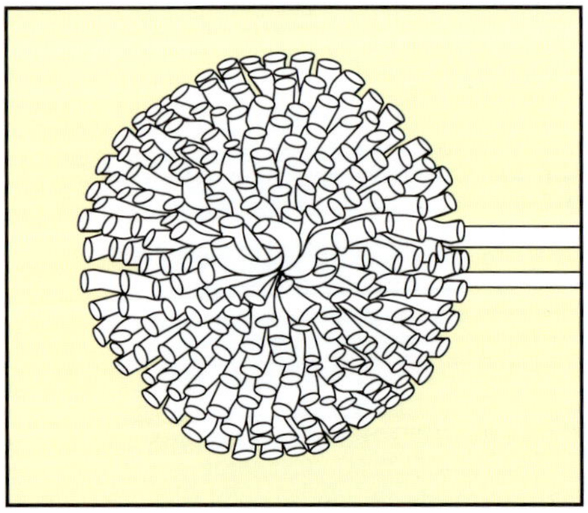

Slouchy Hat

Shown on page 23.

●●○○ EASY

SHOPPING LIST

Yarn (Medium Weight) MEDIUM 4

[5 ounces, 251 yards

(142 grams, 230 meters) per skein]:

- ☐ Dark Brown - 1 skein
- ☐ Yellow - 16 yards (14.5 meters)

See pages 12-17 for colors and yardage of desired features.

Crochet Hook

- ☐ Size H (5 mm)

  or size needed for gauge

Additional Supplies

- ☐ Yarn needle
- ☐ Pin back

GAUGE INFORMATION

Rnds 1-4 = 4¼" (10.75 cm)

14 sc = 4" (10 cm)

Gauge Swatch:

4¼" (10.75 cm) diameter

Work same as Body through Rnd 4: 24 V-Sts.

SIZE INFORMATION

Size: Small{Medium-Large}

19½{20½-21¾}"/49.5{52-55} cm

Size Note: We have printed the instructions for the sizes in different colors to make it easier for you to find:

- Size Small in Blue
- Medium in Pink
- Size Large in Green

Instructions in Black apply to all sizes.

STITCH GUIDE

BEGINNING V-STITCH ***(abbreviated beginning V-St)***

Ch 4 **(counts as first dc plus ch 1)**, dc in same st or sp.

V-STITCH ***(abbreviated V-St)***

(Dc, ch 1, dc) in st or sp indicated.

BODY

With Dark Brown, ch 4; join with slip st to form a ring.

Rnd 1 (Right side)**:** Ch 3 **(counts as first dc, now and throughout)**, 11 dc in ring; join with slip st to first dc: 12 dc.

Rnd 2: Work beginning V-St, work V-St in next dc and in each dc around; join with slip st to first dc: 12 V-Sts.

Rnd 3: Work (slip st, beginning V-St) in next ch-1 sp, work 2 V-Sts in next ch-1 sp, ★ work V-St in next ch-1 sp, work 2 V-Sts in next ch-1 sp; repeat from ★ around; join with slip st to first dc: 18 V-Sts.

Rnd 4: Work (slip st, beginning V-St) in next ch-1 sp, work V-St in next ch-1 sp, work 2 V-Sts in next ch-1 sp, ★ work V-St in next 2 ch-1 sps, work 2 V-Sts in next ch-1 sp; repeat from ★ around; join with slip st to first dc: 24 V-Sts.

Rnd 5: Work (slip st, beginning V-St) in next ch-1 sp, work V-St in next 2 ch-1 sps, work 2 V-Sts in next ch-1 sp, ★ work V-St in next 3 ch-1 sps, work 2 V-Sts in next ch-1 sp; repeat from ★ around; join with slip st to first dc: 30 V-Sts.

Rnd 6: Work (slip st, beginning V-St) in next ch-1 sp,work V-St in next 3 ch-1 sps, work 2 V-Sts in next ch-1 sp, ★ work V-St in next 4 ch-1 sps, work 2 V-Sts in next ch-1 sp; repeat from ★ around; join with slip st to first dc: 36 V-Sts.

Rnd 7: Work (slip st, beginning V-St) in next ch-1 sp, work V-St in next 4 ch-1 sps, work 2 V-Sts in next ch-1 sp, ★ work V-St in next 5 ch-1 sps, work 2 V-Sts in next ch-1 sp; repeat from ★ around; join with slip st to first dc: 42 V-Sts.

Sizes Small & Medium ONLY

Rnd 8: Work (slip st, beginning V-St) in next ch-1 sp, work V-St in next 5 ch-1 sps, work 2 V-Sts in next ch-1 sp, ★ work V-St in next 6 ch-1 sps, work 2 V-Sts in next ch-1 sp; repeat from ★ around; join with slip st to first dc: 48 V-Sts.

Size Large ONLY

Rnd 8: Work (slip st, beginning V-St) in next ch-1 sp, ★ work V-St in next 2 ch-1 sps, work 2 V-Sts in next ch-1 sp; repeat from ★ once **more**, † work V-St in next 6 ch-1 sps, work 2 V-Sts in next ch-1 sp †; repeat from † to † once, work V-St in next 3 ch-1 sps, work 2 V-Sts in next ch-1 sp, work V-St in next 2 ch-1 sps, work 2 V-Sts in next ch-1 sp, repeat from † to † twice; join with slip st to first dc: 50 V-Sts.

All Sizes

Rnds 9 thru 14{14-15}: Work (slip st, beginning V-St) in next ch-1 sp,★ work V-St in next ch-1 sp and in each ch-1 sp around; join with slip st to first dc.

Size Small ONLY

Rnd 15: Slip st in next ch-1 sp, ch 3, dc in next 2 ch-1 sps, 2 dc in next ch-1 sp, (dc in next ch-1 sp, 2 dc in next ch-1 sp) 4 times, ★ dc in next 3 ch-1 sps, 2 dc in next ch-1 sp, (dc in next ch-1 sp, 2 dc in next ch-1 sp) 4 times; repeat from ★ around; join with slip st to first dc: 68 dc.

Size Medium ONLY

Rnd 15: Slip st in next ch-1 sp, ch 3, 2 dc in next ch-1 sp, (dc in next ch-1 sp, 2 dc in next ch-1 sp) around; join with slip st to first dc: 72 dc.

Size Large ONLY

Rnd 16: Slip st in next ch-1 sp, ch 3, dc in same sp, 2 dc in next ch-1 sp, (dc in next ch-1 sp, 2 dc in next ch-1 sp) around; join with slip st to first dc: 76 dc.

BAND

Rnds 1-5: Slip st in sp **before** next dc *(Fig. 5, page 31)*, ch 3, dc in same sp, (skip next 2 dc, 2 dc in sp **before** next dc) around; join with slip st to first dc.

Finish off.

PIN

Make Head and desired Emoji features on pages 11-17.
Sew Features to Head.
Attach pin back to **wrong** side of Emoji. Pin to Hat.

Design by Lisa Gentry.

Tissue Box Cover

●●○○ EASY +

Finished Size: Fits a Boutique Tissue Box

SHOPPING LIST

Yarn (Medium Weight) 4 MEDIUM

[7 ounces, 364 yards (198 grams, 333 meters) per skein]:

☐ Yellow - 1 skein

See pages 12-17 for colors and yardage of desired features.

Crochet Hook

☐ Size H (5 mm)
or size needed for gauge

Additional Supplies

☐ Yarn needle

GAUGE INFORMATION

In pattern,
12 sts = 3¼" (8.25 cm)

Gauge Swatch: 3¼" x 2¾" (8.25 cm x 7 cm)

Ch 13.

Row 1: Sc in second ch from hook, dc in next ch, (sc in next ch, dc in next ch) across: 12 sts.

Rows 2-10: Ch 1, turn; sc in first dc, dc in next sc, (sc in next dc, dc in next sc) across.

Finish off.

SIDES

With Yellow, ch 66; being careful **not** to twist ch, join with slip st to form a ring.

Rnd 1: Ch 1, sc in same ch as joining, dc in next ch, (sc in next ch, dc in next ch) around; join with slip st to first sc: 66 sts.

Rnd 2 (Right side)**:** Ch 3 **(counts as first dc, now and throughout)**, turn; sc in next dc, (dc in next sc, sc in next dc) around; join with slip st to first dc.

Note: Loop a short piece of yarn around any stitch to mark Rnd 2 as **right** side.

Rnd 3: Ch 1, turn; sc in same st as joining, dc in next sc, (sc in next dc, dc in next sc) around; join with slip st to first sc.

Rnds 4-20: Repeat Rnds 2 and 3, 8 times; then repeat Rnd 2 once **more**, do **not** finish off.

TOP

Row 1: Ch 1, turn; working in Front Loops Only *(Fig. 3, page 30)*, sc in same st as joining, (dc in next sc, sc in next dc) 8 times, leave remaining sts unworked: 17 sts.

Row 2: Ch 3, turn; (sc in next dc, dc in next sc) across.

Row 3: Ch 1, turn; sc in first dc, (dc in next sc, sc in next dc) across.

Rows 4-7: Repeat Rows 2 and 3 twice.

Row 8: Ch 3, turn; (sc in next dc, dc in next sc) twice, ch 7 loosely (opening), skip next 7 sts, dc in next sc, (sc in next dc, dc in next sc) twice: 10 sts and 7 chs.

Row 9: Ch 1, turn; sc in first dc, (dc in next sc, sc in next dc) twice, dc in next ch, (sc in next ch, dc in next ch) 3 times, sc in next dc, (dc in next sc, sc in next dc) twice: 17 sts.

Rows 10-15: Repeat Rows 2 and 3, 3 times.

Finish off.

FINISHING

Working in Back Loops Only of Rnd 20 of Sides, sew Top to Sides.

Make desired facial features on pages 12-17; then sew to all Sides.

Design by Lois J. Long.

Organizer

●●○○ EASY +

Finished Size: Fits a Boutique Tissue Box

SHOPPING LIST

Yarn (Medium Weight) MEDIUM 4

[7 ounces, 364 yards (198 grams, 333 meters) per skein]:

- ☐ Grey - 1 skein
- ☐ Yellow - 16 yards (14.5 meters)

See pages 12-17 for colors and yardage of desired features.

Crochet Hook

- ☐ Size H (5 mm)
  or size needed for gauge

Additional Supplies

- ☐ Yarn needle
- ☐ Polyester fiberfill

GAUGE INFORMATION

16 sc and 16 rows = 4" (10 cm)

Gauge Swatch: 4" (10 cm) square

With Grey, ch 17.

Rows 1-16: Work same as Front and Back: 16 sc.

FRONT & BACK

With Grey, ch 17.

Row 1 (Wrong side)**:** Sc in second ch from hook and in each ch across: 16 sc.

Note: Loop a short piece of yarn around **back** of any stitch on Row 1 to mark **right** side.

Rows 2-28: Ch 1, turn; sc in each sc across.

Edging: Ch 1, do **not** turn; 3 sc in last sc on last row; † working in end of rows, skip first row, sc in next row and in each row across to last row, skip last row †; working in free loops of beginning ch *(Fig. 4, page 31)*, 3 sc in ch at base of first sc, sc in each ch across to last ch, 3 sc in last ch; repeat from † to † once; working across sc on last row, 3 sc in first sc, sc in each sc across; join with slip st to first sc, finish off: 92 sc.

SIDE (Make 2)

With Grey, ch 15.

Row 1 (Wrong side)**:** Sc in second ch from hook and in each ch across: 14 sc.

Note: Mark **back** of any stitch on Row 1 as **right** side.

Rows 2-20: Ch 1, turn; sc in each sc across.

Edging: Ch 1, do **not** turn; 3 sc in last sc on Row 20; working in end of rows, skip first row, sc in last 19 rows, working in free loops of beginning ch, 3 sc in ch at base of first sc, sc in each ch across to last ch, 3 sc in last ch; working in end of rows, skip first row, sc in last 19 rows; working across sc on Row 20, 3 sc in first sc, sc in each sc across; join with slip st to first sc, finish off: 74 sc.

RULER POCKET

With Grey, ch 5.

Row 1 (Wrong side)**:** Sc in second ch from hook and in each ch across: 4 sc.

Note: Mark **back** of any stitch on Row 1 as **right** side.

Rows 2-16: Ch 1, turn; sc in each sc across.

Edging: Work same as Front and Back leaving a long end for sewing: 44 sc.

PAD & PEN POCKET

With Grey, ch 15.

Row 1 (Wrong side)**:** Sc in second ch from hook and in each ch across: 14 sc.

Note: Mark **back** of any stitch on Row 1 as **right** side.

Rows 2-18: Ch 1, turn; sc in each sc across.

Edging: Work same as Front and Back leaving a long end for sewing: 68 sc.

HOOKS POCKET

With Grey, ch 15.

Row 1 (Wrong side)**:** Sc in second ch from hook and in each ch across: 14 sc.

Note: Mark **back** of last sc on Row 1 as **right** side and bottom corner (point A).

Rows 2-12: Ch 1, turn; sc in each sc across.

Edging: Ch 1, do **not** turn; 3 sc in last sc on Row 12; working in end of rows, skip first row, sc in next 10 rows, skip last row; working in free loops of beginning ch, 3 sc in ch at base of first sc, sc in last 13 chs; ch 20, (loop to hang markers); skip next 12 rows (top edge); working across sc on Row 12, sc in first 13 sc; join with slip st to first sc, finish off: 42 sc.

SCISSORS POCKET

Row 1: With Grey, ch 2, 2 sc in second ch from hook.

Row 2 (Right side)**:** Ch 1, turn; 2 sc in each of first 2 sc: 4 sc.

Note: Mark Row 2 as **right** side.

Rows 3-12: Ch 1, turn; sc in each sc across.

Row 13: Ch 1, turn; 2 sc in first sc, sc in next 2 sc, 2 sc in last sc: 6 sc.

Row 14: Ch 1, turn; sc in each sc across.

Edging: Ch 1, do **not** turn; 3 sc in last sc on Row 14; working in end of rows, skip first row, sc in next 12 rows, skip last row; 3 sc in free loops of ch at base of first sc; working in end of rows, skip first row, sc in next 12 rows, skip last row; working across sc on Row 14, 3 sc in first sc, sc in last 4 sc; join with slip st to first sc, finish off leaving a long end for sewing: 37 sc.

PINCUSHION

Work Head and Wide Open Eyes, pages 11 and 12.

Using photo on page 27 as a guide for placement and with **right** sides facing:
Sew Eyes to Head.
Using backstitch and Brown, add eyebrows and mouth ***(Fig. 7, page 31)***.

Use diagram as a guide for placement of all pieces.
Sew Scissors Pocket and Ruler Pocket to one Side.
Sew Hooks Pocket to remaining Side.
Sew across every other row from the bottom to top to form six pockets.
Sew Pincushion to Front, stuffing lightly with fiberfill before closing.
Sew Pad & Pencil Pocket to Back.
With **wrong** sides together and working through inside loops, sew Sides to Front and Back.

Design by Theresa Jones.

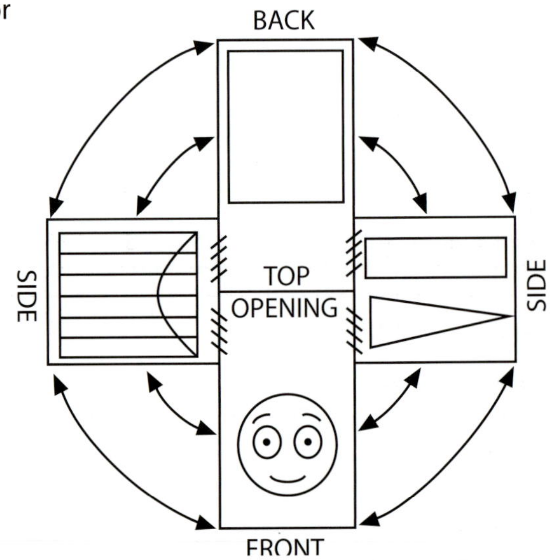

General Instructions

ABBREVIATIONS

ch(s)	chain(s)
cm	centimeters
dc	double crochet(s)
hdc	half double crochet(s)
mm	millimeters
Rnd(s)	Round(s)
sc	single crochet(s)
sp(s)	space(s)
st(s)	stitch(es)
YO	yarn over

SYMBOLS & TERMS

★ — work instructions following ★ as many **more** times as indicated in addition to the first time.

† to † — work all instructions from first † to second † **as many** times as specified.

( ) or [ ] — work enclosed instructions **as many** times as specified by the number immediately following **or** work all enclosed instructions in the stitch or space indicated **or** contains explanatory remarks.

colon (:) — the number(s) given after a colon at the end of a row or round denote(s) the number of stitches you should have on that row or round.

CROCHET TERMINOLOGY		
UNITED STATES		INTERNATIONAL
slip stitch (slip st)	=	single crochet (sc)
single crochet (sc)	=	double crochet (dc)
half double crochet (hdc)	=	half treble crochet (htr)
double crochet (dc)	=	treble crochet (tr)
treble crochet (tr)	=	double treble crochet (dtr)
double treble crochet (dtr)	=	triple treble crochet (ttr)
triple treble crochet (tr tr)	=	quadruple treble crochet (qtr)
skip	=	miss

Yarn Weight Symbol & Names	LACE 0	SUPER FINE 1	FINE 2	LIGHT 3	MEDIUM 4	BULKY 5	SUPER BULKY 6	JUMBO 7
Type of Yarns in Category	Fingering, size 10 crochet thread	Sock, Fingering, Baby	Sport, Baby	DK, Light Worsted	Worsted, Afghan, Aran	Chunky, Craft, Rug	Super Bulky, Roving	Jumbo, Roving
Crochet Gauge* Ranges in Single Crochet to 4" (10 cm)	32-42 sts**	21-32 sts	16-20 sts	12-17 sts	11-14 sts	8-11 sts	6-9 sts	5 sts and fewer
Advised Hook Size Range	Steel*** 6 to 8, Regular hook B-1	B-1 to E-4	E-4 to 7	7 to I-9	I-9 to K-10½	K-10½ to M/N-13	M/N-13 to Q	Q and larger

*GUIDELINES ONLY: The chart above reflects the most commonly used gauges and hook sizes for specific yarn categories.

** Lace weight yarns are usually crocheted with larger hooks to create lacy openwork patterns. Accordingly, a gauge range is difficult to determine. Always follow the gauge stated in your pattern.

*** Steel crochet hooks are sized differently from regular hooks–the higher the number, the smaller the hook, which is the reverse of regular hook sizing.

GAUGE

Exact gauge is **essential** for proper size. Before beginning your project, make the sample swatch given in the individual instructions in the yarn and hook specified. After completing the swatch, measure it, counting your stitches and rows carefully. If your swatch is larger or smaller than specified, **make another, changing hook size to get the correct gauge.** Keep trying until you find the size hook that will give you the specified gauge.

CROCHET HOOKS																	
U.S.	B-1	C-2	D-3	E-4	F-5	G-6	7	H-8	I-9	J-10	K-10½	L-11	M/N-13	N/P-15	P/Q	Q	S
Metric - mm	2.25	2.75	3.25	3.5	3.75	4	4.5	5	5.5	6	6.5	8	9	10	15	16	19

●○○○ **BEGINNER**	Projects for first-time crocheters using basic stitches. Minimal shaping.
●●○○ **EASY**	Projects using yarn with basic stitches, repetitive stitch patterns, simple color changes, and simple shaping and finishing.
●●●○ **INTERMEDIATE**	Projects using a variety of techniques, such as basic lace patterns or color patterns, mid-level shaping and finishing.
●●●● **EXPERIENCED**	Projects with intricate stitch patterns, techniques and dimension, such as non-repeating patterns, multi-color techniques, fine threads, small hooks, detailed shaping and refined finishing.

MARKERS

Markers are used to help distinguish the beginning of each round being worked. Place a 2" (5 cm) scrap piece of yarn before the first stitch of each round, moving the marker after each round is complete.

JOINING WITH SC

When instructed to join with sc, begin with a slip knot on hook. Insert hook in stitch or space indicated, YO and pull up a loop, YO and draw through both loops on hook.

ADJUSTABLE LOOP

Wind the yarn around two fingers to form a ring *(Fig. 1a)*, slide the yarn off your fingers and grasp the strands at the top to the ring *(Fig. 1b)*. Insert the hook from **front** to **back** into the ring, pull up a loop, YO and draw through the loop on hook to lock the ring *(Fig. 1c)*.

Working around **both** strands, work stitches in the ring as specified, then pull the yarn end to close *(Fig. 1d)*.

Fig. 1a

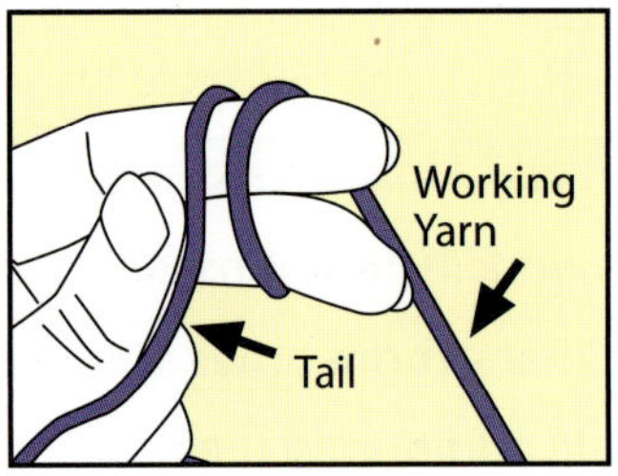

Fig. 1b

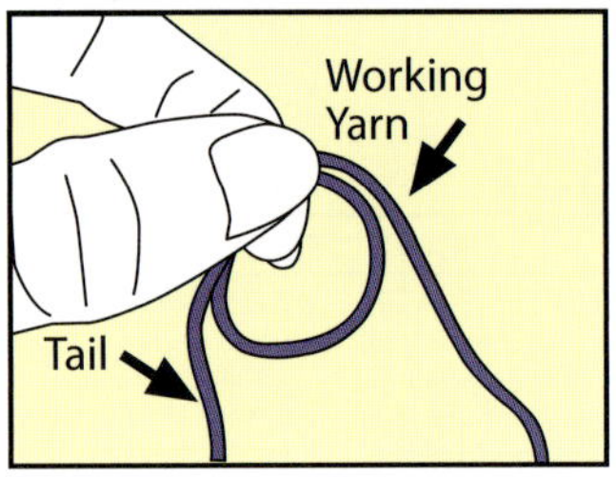

Fig. 1c

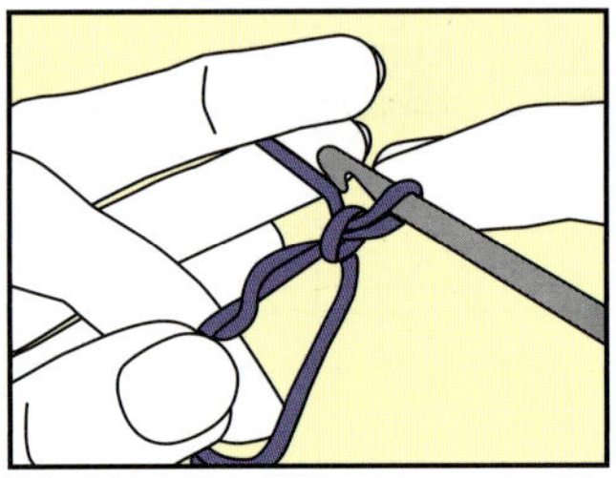

Fig. 1d

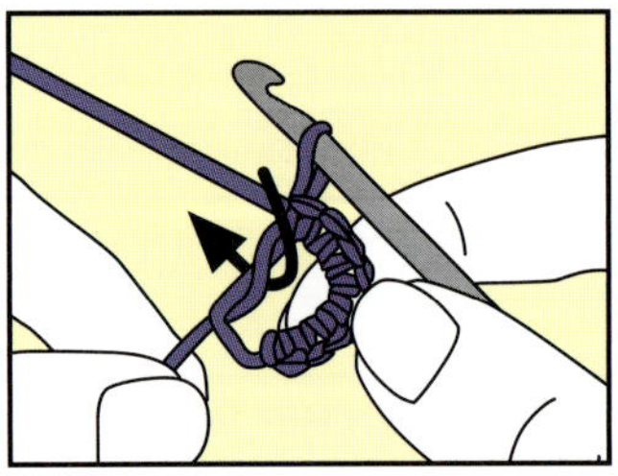

BACK RIDGE OF A CHAIN

Work only in loops indicated by arrows *(Fig. 2)*.

Fig. 2

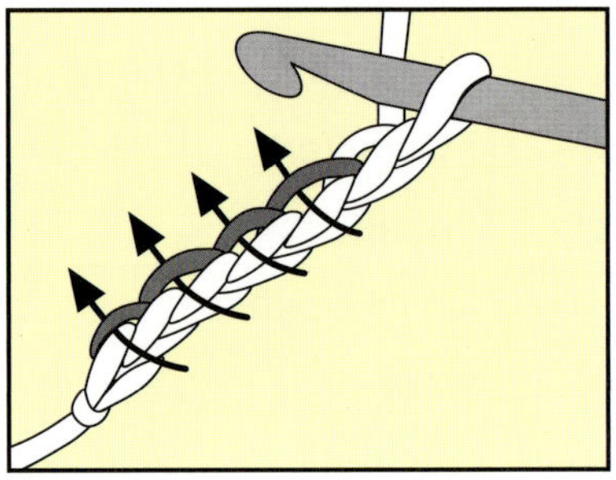

BACK OR FRONT LOOPS ONLY

Work only in loop(s) indicated by arrow *(Fig. 3)*.

Fig. 3

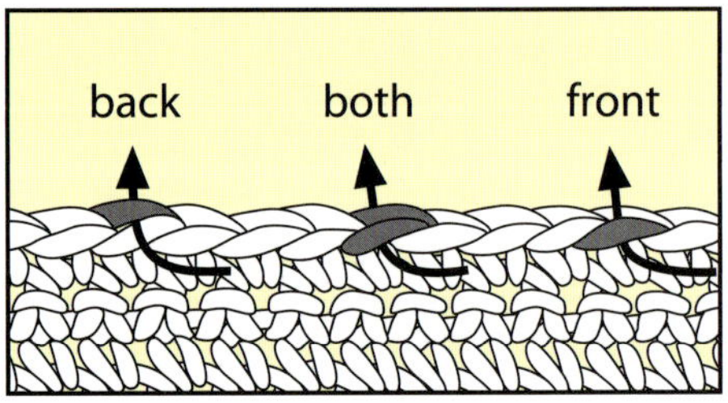

FREE LOOPS

When instructed to work in free loops of a chain, work in loop indicated by arrow *(Fig. 4)*.

Fig. 4

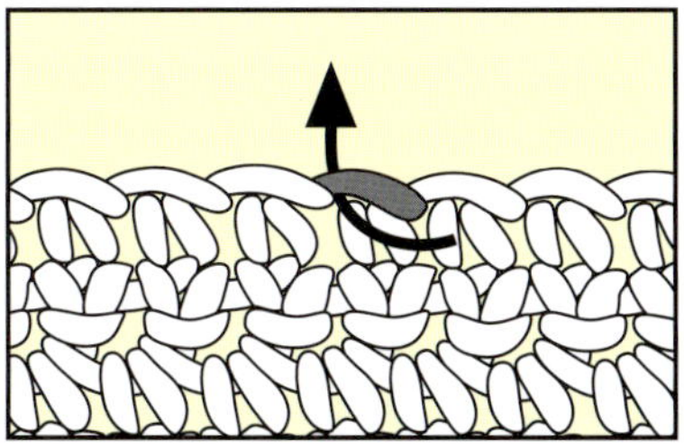

WORKING IN A SPACE BEFORE A STITCH

When instructed to work in a space **before** a stitch or in spaces **between** stitches, insert hook in space indicated by arrow *(Fig. 5)*.

Fig. 5

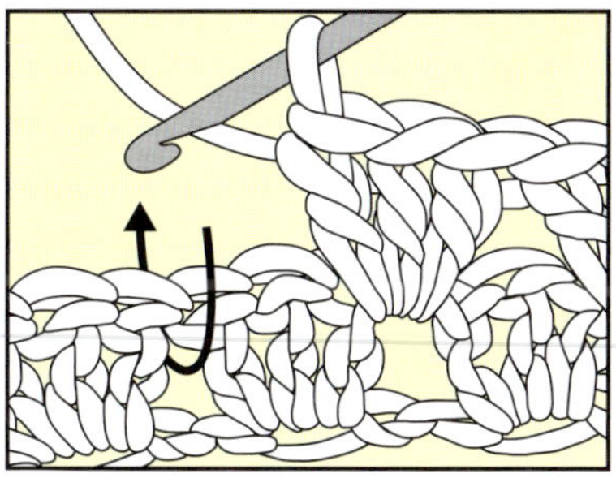

WHIPSTITCH

With **wrong** sides together, sew through both pieces once to secure the beginning of the seam, leaving an ample yarn end to weave in later. Insert the needle from **back** to **front** through **both** loops on **both** pieces *(Fig. 6)*. Bring the needle around and insert it from **back** to **front** through the next loops of both pieces. Continue in this manner across to corner, keeping the sewing yarn fairly loose.

Fig. 6

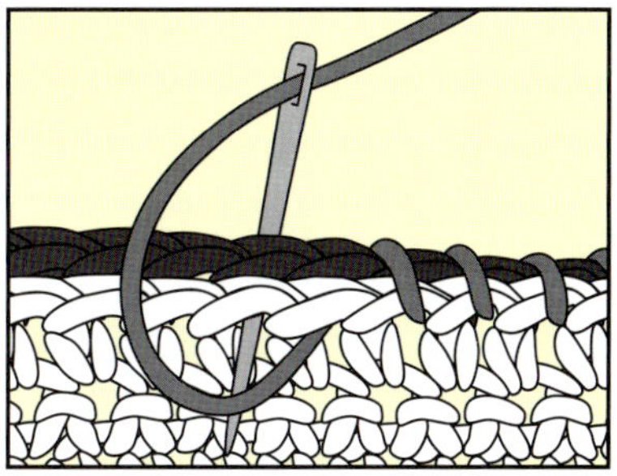

BACKSTITCH

The backstitch is worked from **right** to **left**. Come up at 1, go down at 2 and come up at 3 *(Fig. 7)*. The second stitch is made by going down at 1 and coming up at 4.

Fig. 7

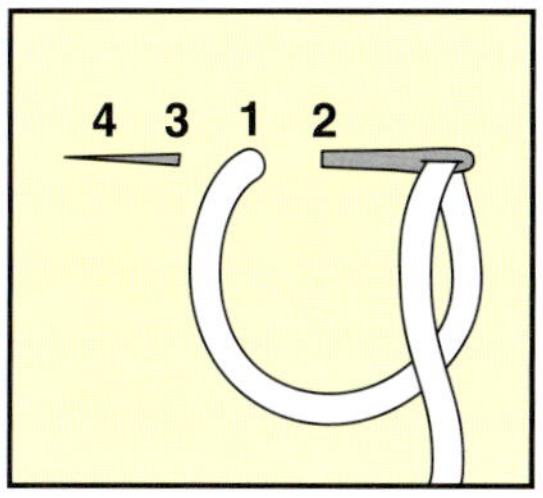

Yarn Information

The items in this book were made using Medium or Light Weight Yarn. Any brand of the specified weight of yarn may be used. It is best to refer to the yardage/meters when determining how many balls or skeins to purchase. Remember, to arrive at the finished size, it is the GAUGE/TENSION that is important, not the brand of yarn.

For your convenience, listed below are the specific yarns used to create our photography models. Because yarn manufacturers make frequent changes in their product lines, you may sometimes find it necessary to use a substitute yarn or to search for the discontinued product at alternate suppliers (locally or online).

FACES

Red Heart® With Love®
Dark Blue - #1814 True Blue
Red Heart® Super Saver®
Yellow - #235 Lemon
Lion Brand® Vanna's Choice®
Brown - #124 Toffee
Black - #153 Black
Blue - #108 Bluebell
White - #100 White
Pink - #138 Pink Poodle
Dark Pink - #112 Raspberry
Grey - #149 Silver Grey

BLANKET

Red Heart® With Love®
Dark Blue - #1814 True Blue
Brown - #1321 Chocolate
Pink - #1704 Bubble Gum
Blue - #1805 Bluebell
Black - #1012 Black
White - #1001 White
Dark Pink - #1701 Hot Pink
Red Heart® Super Saver®
Yellow - #235 Lemon

SCARF

Caron® Simply Soft® Light™
Dark Blue - #0008 Riviera
Yellow - #0003 Honey
Brown - #0019 Taupe

DESIGN A FACE

Red Heart® Super Saver®
Yellow - #235 Lemon
Lion Brand® Vanna's Choice®
Brown - #124 Toffee
Blue - #108 Bluebell
White - #100 White
Dark Pink - #112 Raspberry
Pink - #138 Pink Poodle
Grey - #149 Silver Grey

BEANIE

Lion Brand® Pound of Love®
Yellow - #158 Honey Bee
Lion Brand® Vanna's Choice®
Brown - #124 Toffee

SLOUCHY HAT

Lion Brand® Heartland®
Dark Brown - #126 Sequoia
Red Heart® Super Saver®
Yellow - #235 Lemon
Lion Brand® Vanna's Choice®
Brown - #124 Toffee

TISSUE BOX COVER

Red Heart® Super Saver®
Yellow - #235 Lemon
Lion Brand® Vanna's Choice®
Brown - #124 Toffee
Dark Pink - #112 Raspberry
White - #100 White

ORGANIZER

Red Heart® Super Saver®
Grey - #3950 Charcoal
Yellow - #235 Lemon
Lion Brand® Vanna's Choice®
Brown - #124 Toffee
White - #100 White

We have made every effort to ensure that these instructions are accurate and complete. We cannot, however, be responsible for human error, typographical mistakes, or variations in individual work.

Production Team: Instructional/Technical Writer - Lois J. Long; Editorial Writer - Susan Frantz Wiles; Senior Graphic Artist - Lora Puls; Graphic Artist - Victoria Temple; Photo Stylist - Lori Wenger; and Photographer - Jason Masters.

Items made and instructions tested by Janet Akins and Raymelle Greening.